HAL•LEONARD

INSTRUMENTAL PLAY-ALONG

AUDIO ACCESS INCLUDED

PLAYBACK+
Speed • Pitch • Balance • Loop

THE GREATEST SHOWMAN

Come Alive...2

From Now On...3

The Greatest Show 4

A Million Dreams 5

Never Enough...6

The Other Side 8

Rewrite the Stars 9

This Is Me 10

Tightrope..12

Audio Arrangements by Peter Deneff

To access audio visit:
www.halleonard.com/mylibrary
Enter Code
4445-3992-0339-4288

ISBN 978-1-5400-2847-1

HAL•LEONARD®

7777 W. BLUEMOUND RD. P.O. BOX 13819 MILWAUKEE, WI 53213

In Australia Contact:
Hal Leonard Australia Pty. Ltd.
4 Lentara Court
Cheltenham, Victoria, 3192 Australia
Email: ausadmin@halleonard.com.au

Visit Hal Leonard Online at
www.halleonard.com

COME ALIVE

VIOLIN

Words and Music by BENJ PASEK
and JUSTIN PAUL

FROM NOW ON

VIOLIN

Words and Music by BENJ PASEK
and JUSTIN PAUL

THE GREATEST SHOW

VIOLIN

Words and Music by BENJ PASEK, JUSTIN PAUL and RYAN LEWIS

A MILLION DREAMS

VIOLIN

Words and Music by BENJ PASEK
and JUSTIN PAUL

NEVER ENOUGH

VIOLIN

Words and Music by BENJ PASEK
and JUSTIN PAUL

THE OTHER SIDE

VIOLIN

Words and Music by BENJ PASEK
and JUSTIN PAUL

REWRITE THE STARS

VIOLIN

Words and Music by BENJ PASEK
and JUSTIN PAUL

THIS IS ME

VIOLIN

Words and Music by BENJ PASEK
and JUSTIN PAUL

TIGHTROPE

VIOLIN

Words and Music by BENJ PASEK
and JUSTIN PAUL